NAT TURNER'S
REBELLION

BY SHAWN PRYOR

ILLUSTRATED BY SILVIO DB

CONSULTANT:
JAMES DIMOCK,
PROFESSOR OF COMMUNICATION STUDIES
MINNESOTA STATE UNIVERSITY, MANKATO

CAPSTONE PRESS
a capstone imprint

Graphic Library is published by Capstone Press, an imprint of Capstone.
1710 Roe Crest Drive
North Mankato, Minnesota 56003
www.capstonepub.com

Library of Congress Cataloging-in-Publication Data is available
on the Library of Congress website.

ISBN: 978-1-4966-8122-5 (library binding)
ISBN: 978-1-4966-8685-5 (paperback)
ISBN: 978-1-4966-8158-4 (eBook PDF)

Summary: Nat Turner, an enslaved black man, believed he was chosen by
God to battle against the evils of slavery. Driven by visions, Turner banded
with other enslaved people, and on August 21, 1831, his rebellion began with
attacks at plantations in Southampton, Virginia. As he and his group moved
from plantation to plantation, dozens of enslaved men joined them,
until the local militia put an end to their rebellion.

Editorial Credits
Editor: Julie Gassman; Designer: Tracy McCabe;
Media Researcher: Eric Gohl; Production Specialist: Laura Manthe

All internet sites appearing in back matter were available and
accurate when this book was sent to press.

Printed in the United States of America.
PA117

TABLE OF CONTENTS

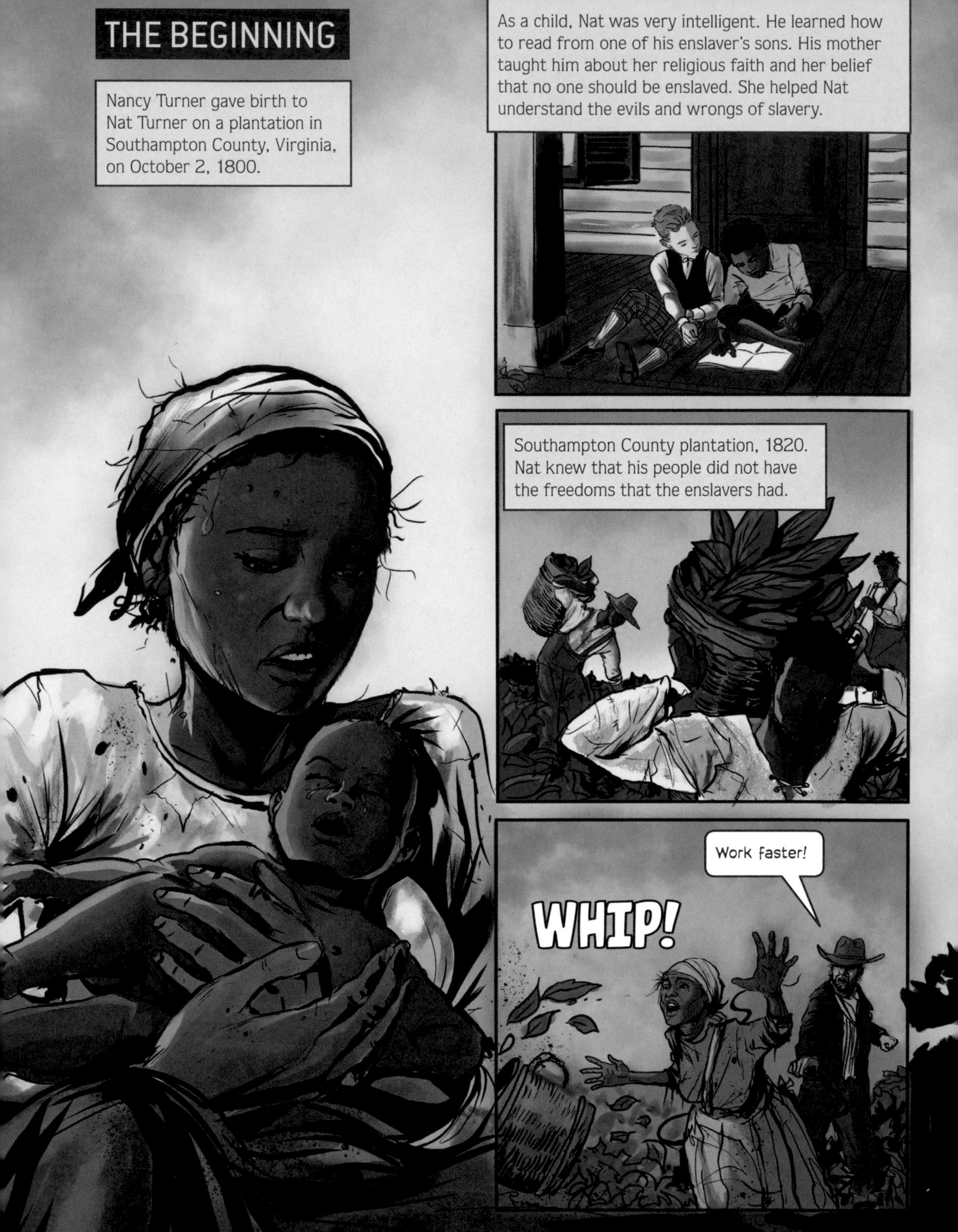
THE BEGINNING
Nancy Turner gave birth to Nat Turner on a plantation in Southampton County, Virginia, on October 2, 1800.
As a child, Nat was very intelligent. He learned how to read from one of his enslaver's sons. His mother taught him about her religious faith and her belief that no one should be enslaved. She helped Nat understand the evils and wrongs of slavery.
Southampton County plantation, 1820. Nat knew that his people did not have the freedoms that the enslavers had.
Work faster!
WHIP!

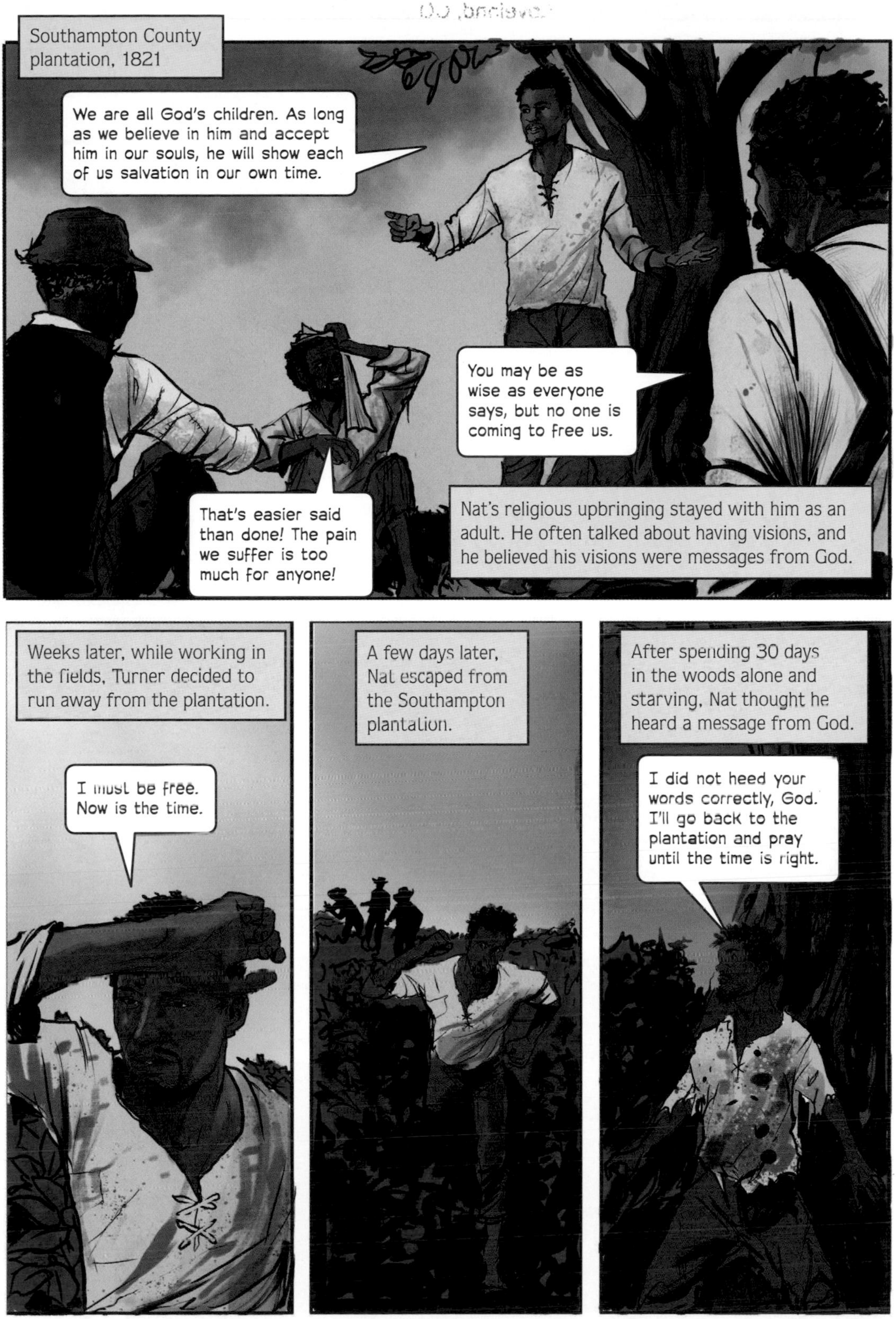
Southampton County plantation, 1821
We are all God's children. As long as we believe in him and accept him in our souls, he will show each of us salvation in our own time.
You may be as wise as everyone says, but no one is coming to free us.
That's easier said than done! The pain we suffer is too much for anyone!
Nat's religious upbringing stayed with him as an adult. He often talked about having visions, and he believed his visions were messages from God.
Weeks later, while working in the fields, Turner decided to run away from the plantation.
I must be free. Now is the time.
A few days later, Nat escaped from the Southampton plantation.
After spending 30 days in the woods alone and starving, Nat thought he heard a message from God.
I did not heed your words correctly, God. I'll go back to the plantation and pray until the time is right.

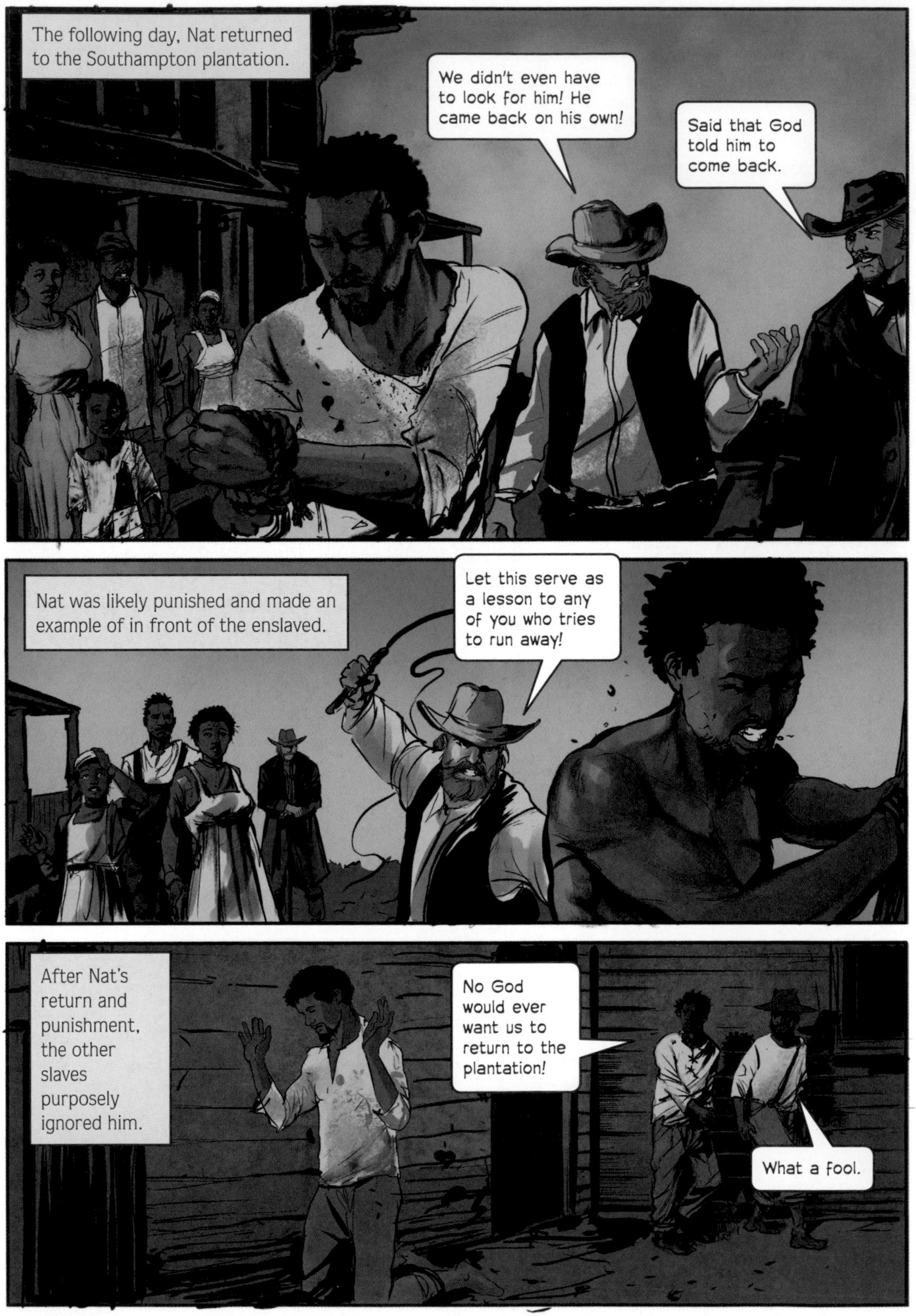
The following day, Nat returned to the Southampton plantation.
We didn't even have to look for him! He came back on his own!
Said that God told him to come back.
Nat was likely punished and made an example of in front of the enslaved.
Let this serve as a lesson to any of you who tries to run away!
After Nat's return and punishment, the other slaves purposely ignored him.
No God would ever want us to return to the plantation!
What a fool.

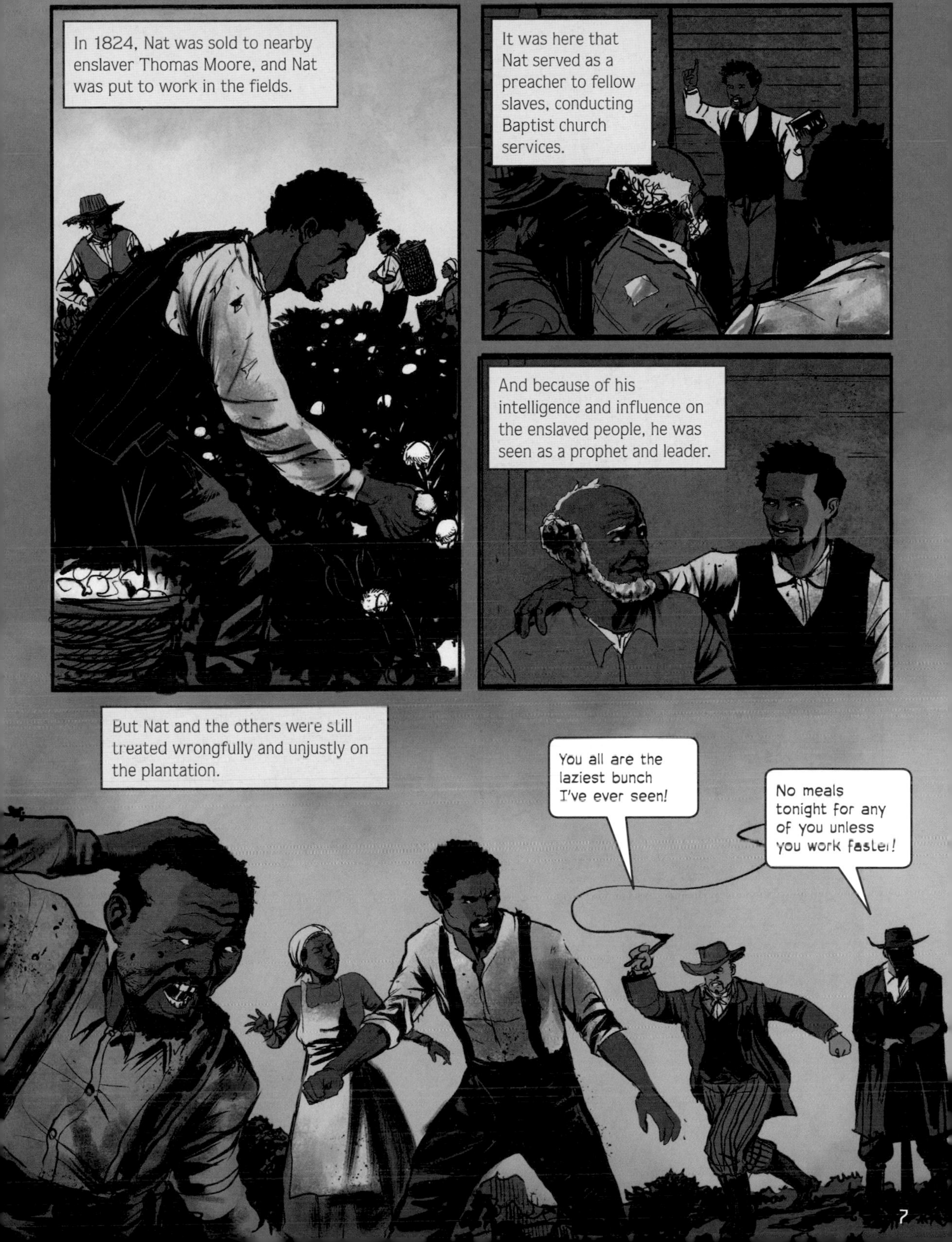
In 1824, Nat was sold to nearby enslaver Thomas Moore, and Nat was put to work in the fields.
It was here that Nat served as a preacher to fellow slaves, conducting Baptist church services.
And because of his intelligence and influence on the enslaved people, he was seen as a prophet and leader.
But Nat and the others were still treated wrongfully and unjustly on the plantation.
You all are the laziest bunch I've ever seen!
No meals tonight for any of you unless you work faster!

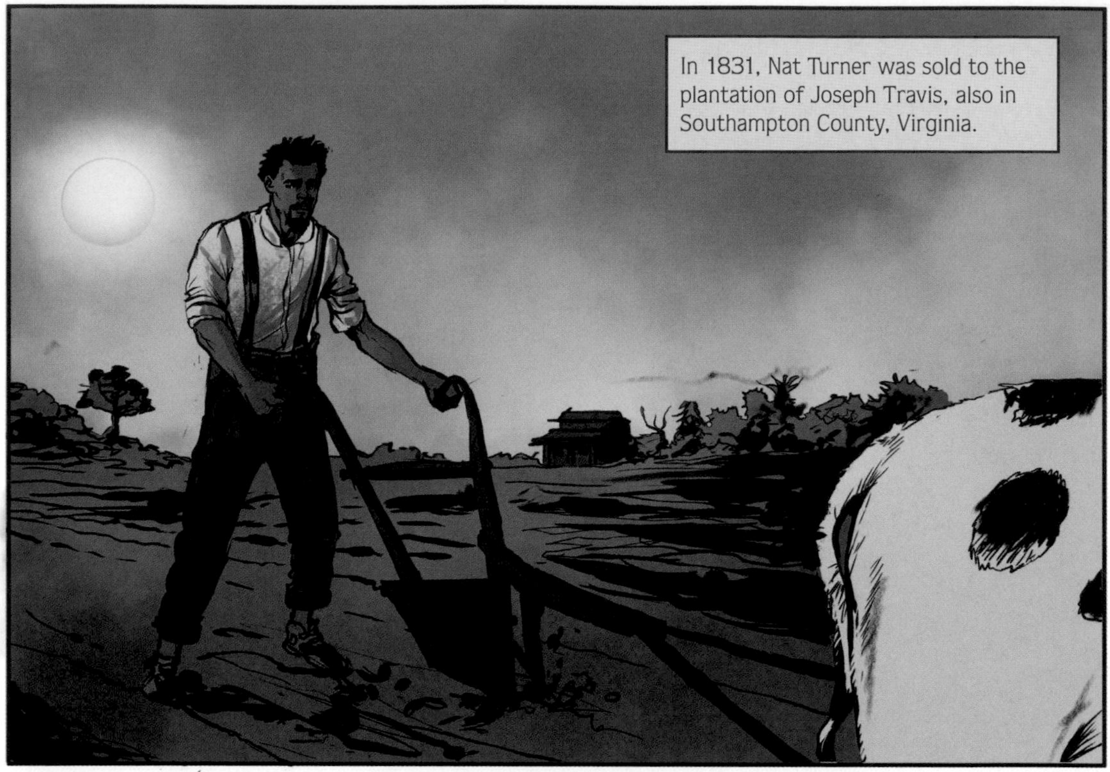
In 1831, Nat Turner was sold to the plantation of Joseph Travis, also in Southampton County, Virginia.

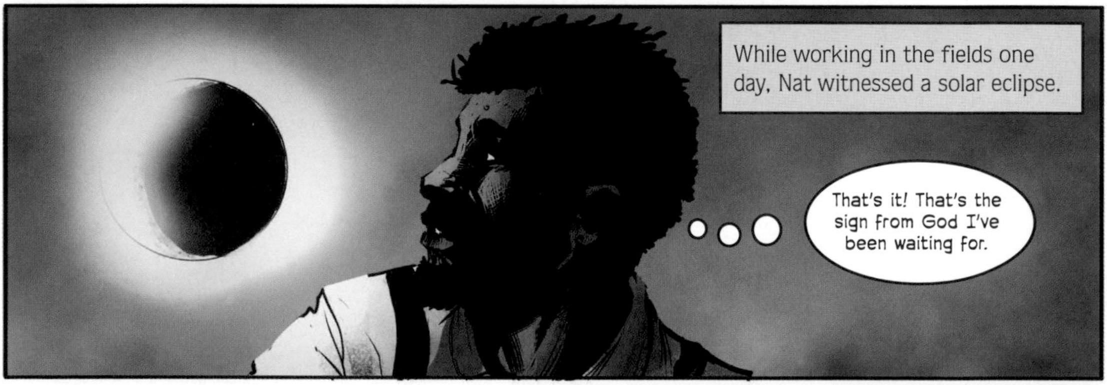
While working in the fields one day, Nat witnessed a solar eclipse.
That's it! That's the sign from God I've been waiting for.

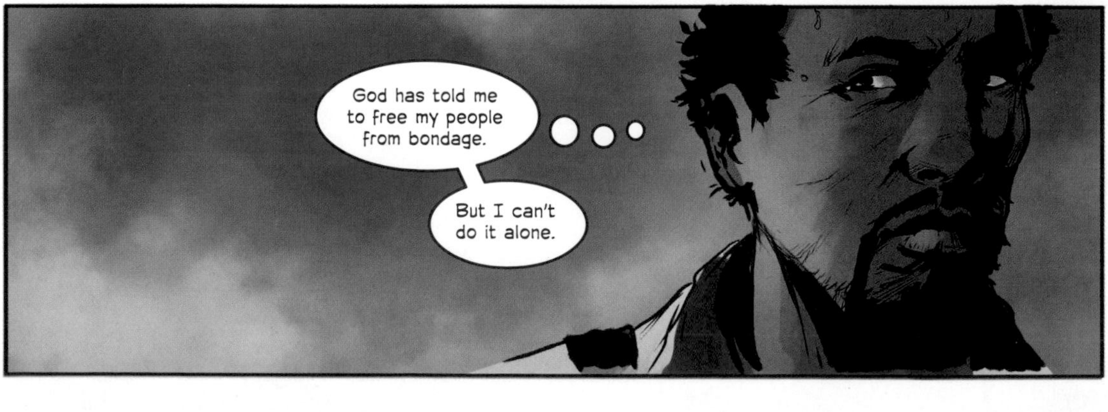
God has told me to free my people from bondage.
But I can't do it alone.

CREATING A REBELLION

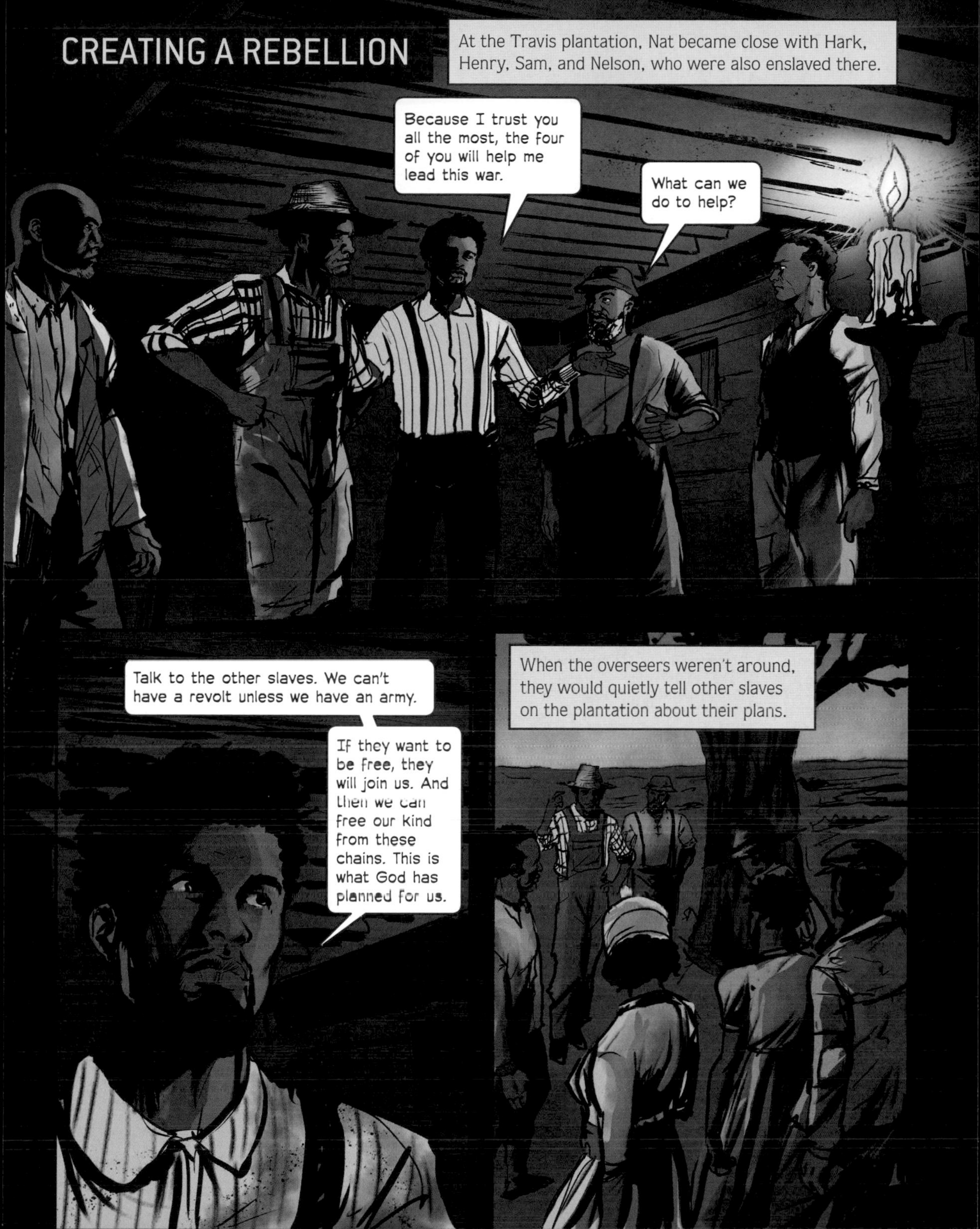
At the Travis plantation, Nat became close with Hark, Henry, Sam, and Nelson, who were also enslaved there.
Because I trust you all the most, the four of you will help me lead this war.
What can we do to help?
Talk to the other slaves. We can't have a revolt unless we have an army.
If they want to be free, they will join us. And then we can free our kind from these chains. This is what God has planned for us.
When the overseers weren't around, they would quietly tell other slaves on the plantation about their plans.

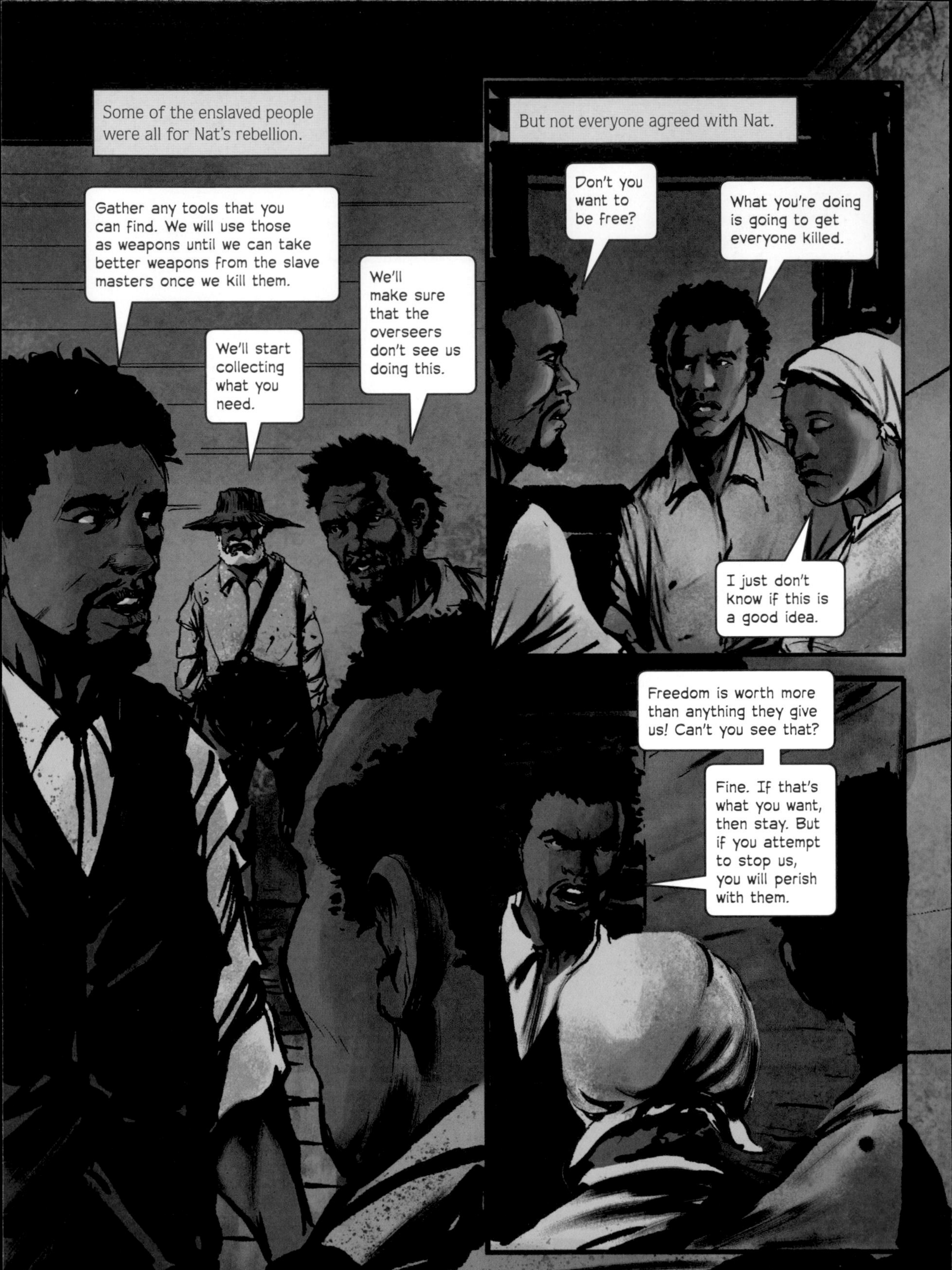
Some of the enslaved people were all for Nat's rebellion.
Gather any tools that you can find. We will use those as weapons until we can take better weapons from the slave masters once we kill them.
We'll start collecting what you need.
We'll make sure that the overseers don't see us doing this.
But not everyone agreed with Nat.
Don't you want to be free?
What you're doing is going to get everyone killed.
I just don't know if this is a good idea.
Freedom is worth more than anything they give us! Can't you see that?
Fine. If that's what you want, then stay. But if you attempt to stop us, you will perish with them.

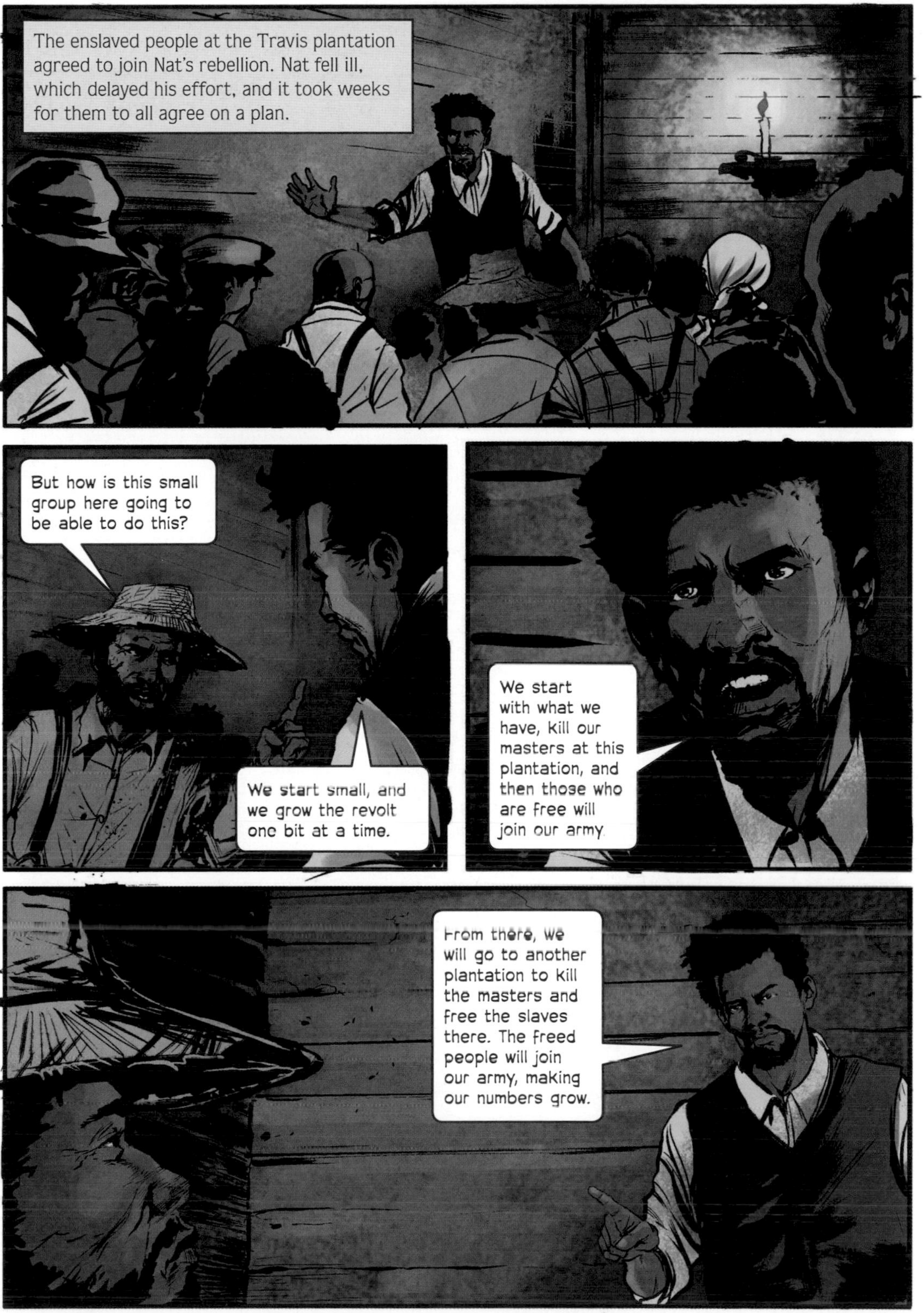
The enslaved people at the Travis plantation agreed to join Nat's rebellion. Nat fell ill, which delayed his effort, and it took weeks for them to all agree on a plan.
But how is this small group here going to be able to do this?
We start small, and we grow the revolt one bit at a time.
We start with what we have, kill our masters at this plantation, and then those who are free will join our army.
From there, we will go to another plantation to kill the masters and free the slaves there. The freed people will join our army, making our numbers grow.

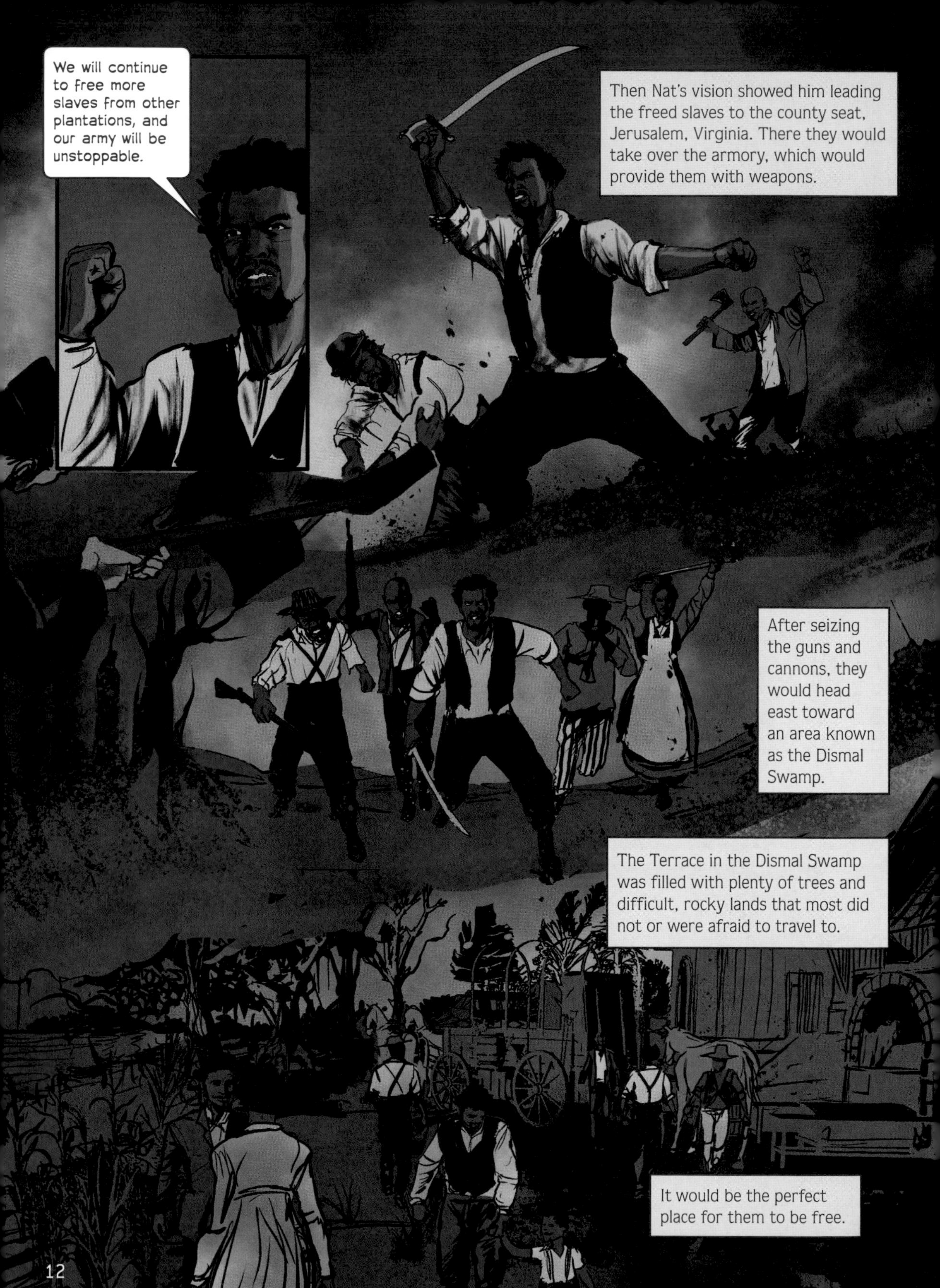
We will continue to free more slaves from other plantations, and our army will be unstoppable.
Then Nat's vision showed him leading the freed slaves to the county seat, Jerusalem, Virginia. There they would take over the armory, which would provide them with weapons.
After seizing the guns and cannons, they would head east toward an area known as the Dismal Swamp.
The Terrace in the Dismal Swamp was filled with plenty of trees and difficult, rocky lands that most did not or were afraid to travel to.
It would be the perfect place for them to be free.

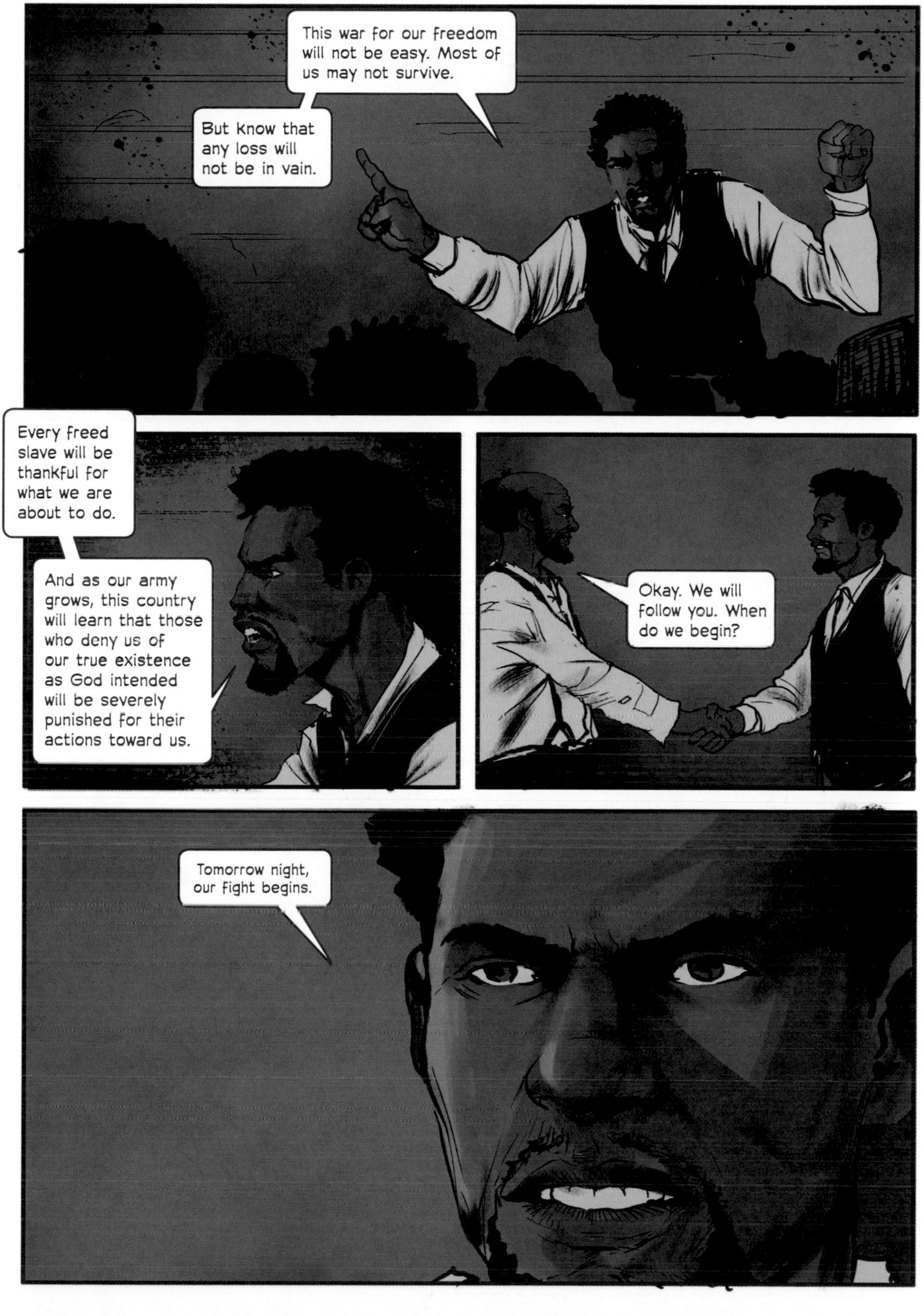
This war for our freedom will not be easy. Most of us may not survive.
But know that any loss will not be in vain.
Every freed slave will be thankful for what we are about to do.
And as our army grows, this country will learn that those who deny us of our true existence as God intended will be severely punished for their actions toward us.
Okay. We will follow you. When do we begin?
Tomorrow night, our fight begins.

THE REBELLION

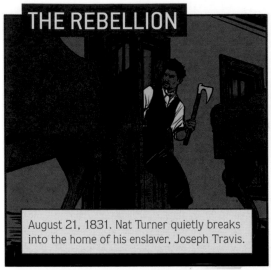

August 21, 1831. Nat Turner quietly breaks into the home of his enslaver, Joseph Travis.

Quiet, everyone. Will and Henry, follow me. The rest of you, look for weapons.

Nat and Will entered the bedroom of Mr. and Mrs. Travis as they slept.

That night, the rebels killed every member of the Travis family on the plantation, and the rebellion began.

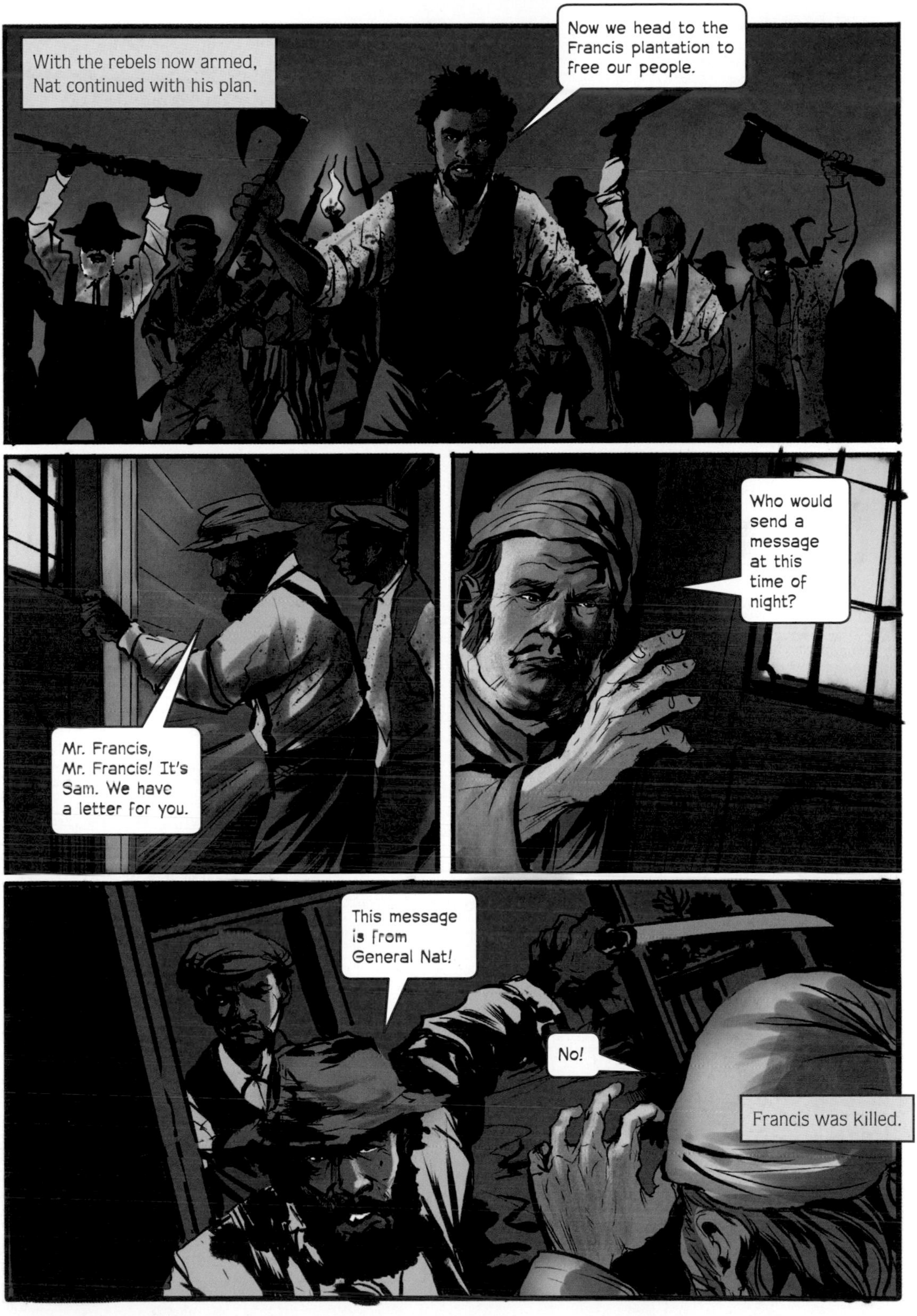
With the rebels now armed, Nat continued with his plan.
Now we head to the Francis plantation to free our people.
Mr. Francis, Mr. Francis! It's Sam. We have a letter for you.
Who would send a message at this time of night?
This message is from General Nat!
No!
Francis was killed.

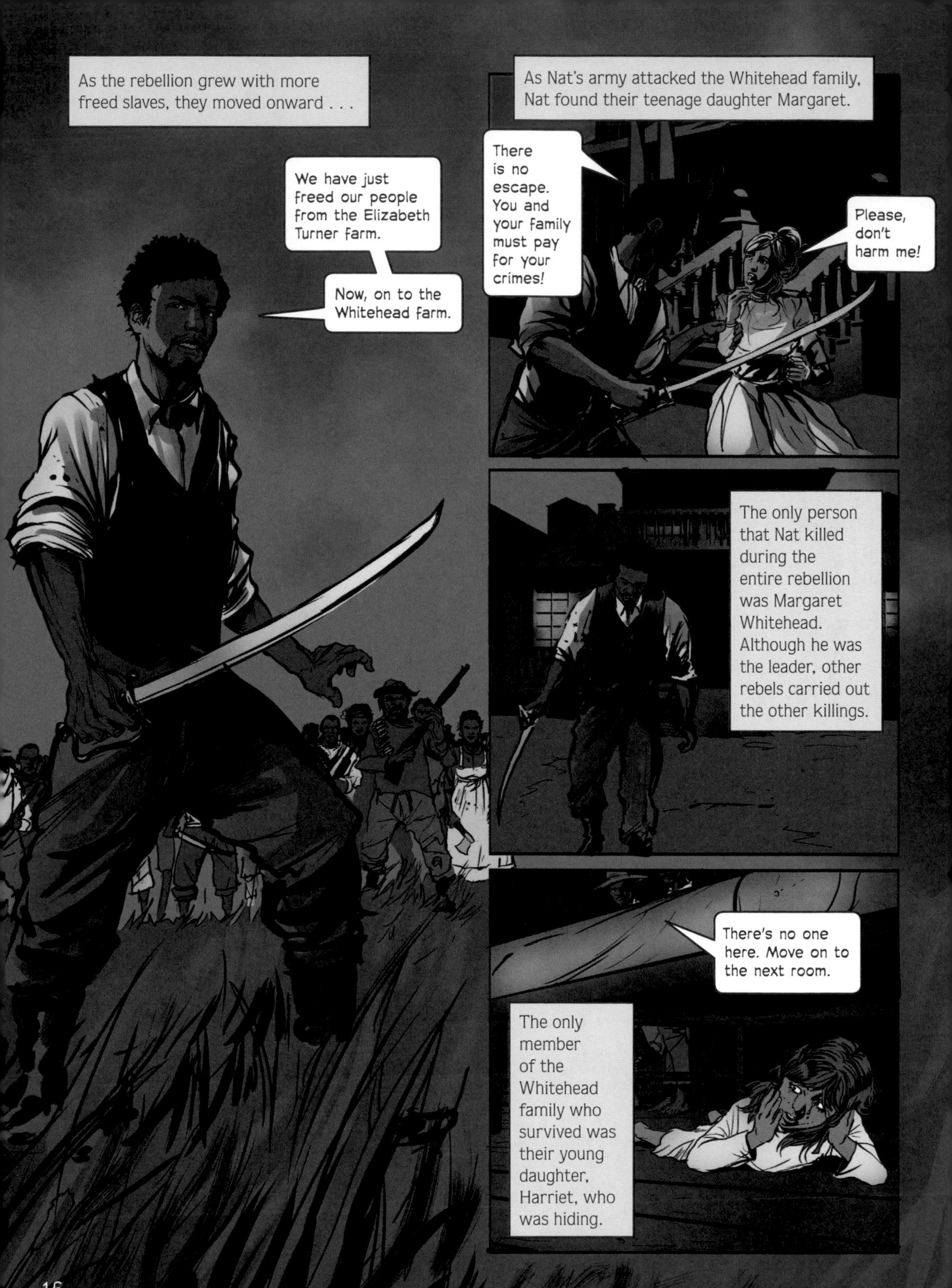
As the rebellion grew with more freed slaves, they moved onward . . .
We have just freed our people from the Elizabeth Turner farm.
Now, on to the Whitehead farm.
As Nat's army attacked the Whitehead family, Nat found their teenage daughter Margaret.
There is no escape. You and your family must pay for your crimes!
Please, don't harm me!
The only person that Nat killed during the entire rebellion was Margaret Whitehead. Although he was the leader, other rebels carried out the other killings.
There's no one here. Move on to the next room.
The only member of the Whitehead family who survived was their young daughter, Harriet, who was hiding.

As the rebellion continued, many plantations feared the enslaved people would realize the power they could have by fighting back.

So the overseers made sure to instill even more fear into those who thought of rebelling from their enslavers.

Let this serve as a lesson for anyone who even thinks about trying to be free!

WHIP! WHIP! WHIP!

As the rebellion continued to grow, news of it spread like wildfire.

These slaves have an army and are killing white people!

We must form a militia in order to put a stop to this, immediately, before it's too late!

Nat Turner's army grew to more than 70 men, all under his command, with more to come as they continued to free their people.

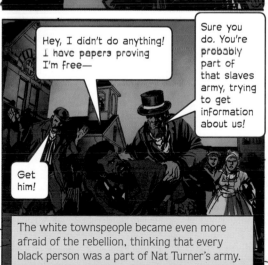

Hey, I didn't do anything! I have papers proving I'm free—

Sure you do. You're probably part of that slaves army, trying to get information about us!

Get him!

The white townspeople became even more afraid of the rebellion, thinking that every black person was a part of Nat Turner's army.

Within 24 hours after the rebellion had begun, a white militia was formed and ready to attack.

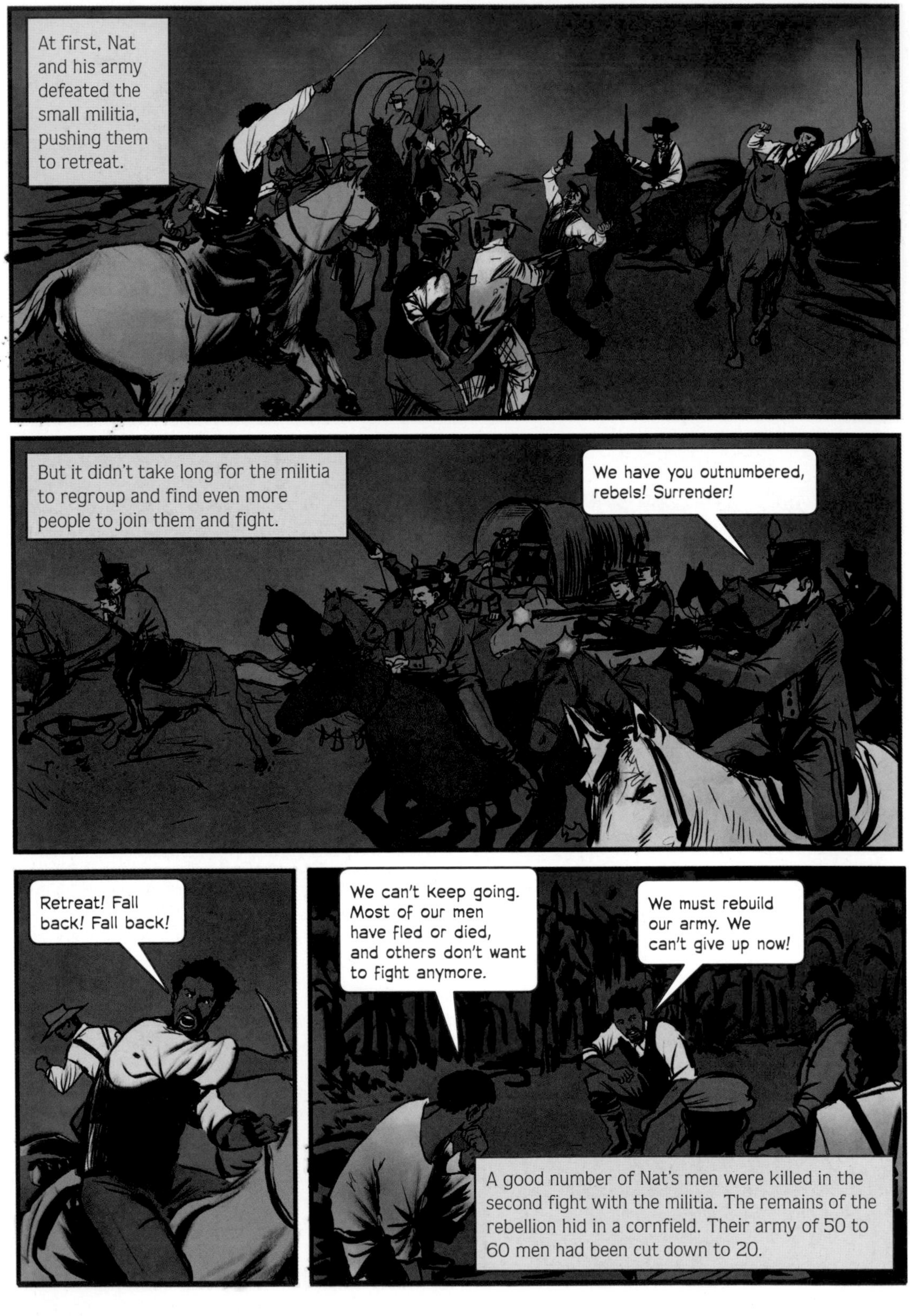
At first, Nat and his army defeated the small militia, pushing them to retreat.
But it didn't take long for the militia to regroup and find even more people to join them and fight.
We have you outnumbered, rebels! Surrender!
Retreat! Fall back! Fall back!
We can't keep going. Most of our men have fled or died, and others don't want to fight anymore.
We must rebuild our army. We can't give up now!
A good number of Nat's men were killed in the second fight with the militia. The remains of the rebellion hid in a cornfield. Their army of 50 to 60 men had been cut down to 20.

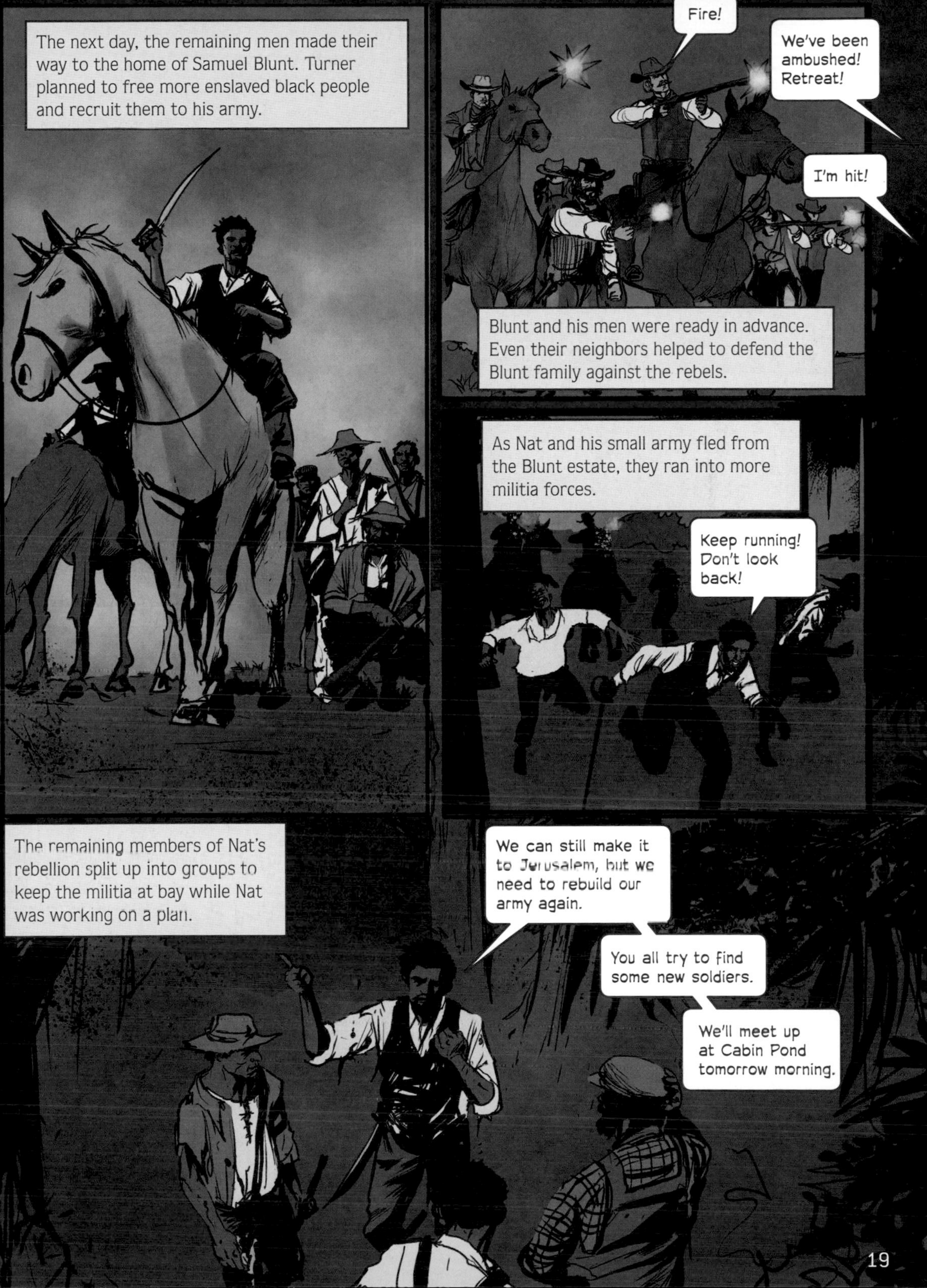

The next day, the remaining men made their way to the home of Samuel Blunt. Turner planned to free more enslaved black people and recruit them to his army.
Fire!
We've been ambushed! Retreat!
I'm hit!
Blunt and his men were ready in advance. Even their neighbors helped to defend the Blunt family against the rebels.
As Nat and his small army fled from the Blunt estate, they ran into more militia forces.
Keep running! Don't look back!
The remaining members of Nat's rebellion split up into groups to keep the militia at bay while Nat was working on a plan.
We can still make it to Jerusalem, but we need to rebuild our army again.
You all try to find some new soldiers.
We'll meet up at Cabin Pond tomorrow morning.

The next day, Nat waited for his men to return. No one showed up.

Where is everyone?

The surviving men in his army were either captured, killed, or ran away.

Stories of the rebellion grew around southeast Virginia, adding panic to the fear and anger of the white people who lived there.

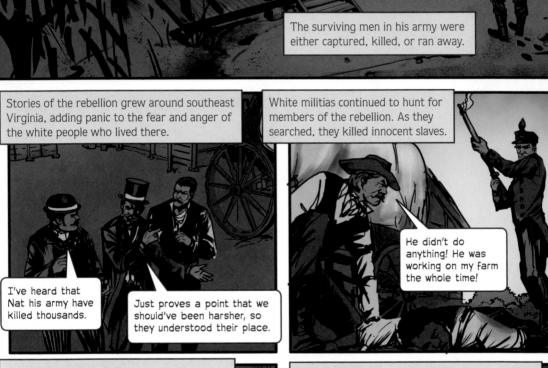

I've heard that Nat his army have killed thousands.

Just proves a point that we should've been harsher, so they understood their place.

White militias continued to hunt for members of the rebellion. As they searched, they killed innocent slaves.

He didn't do anything! He was working on my farm the whole time!

Newspaper reporters such as John Hampden Pleasants argued with white people over what was happening during the rebellion.

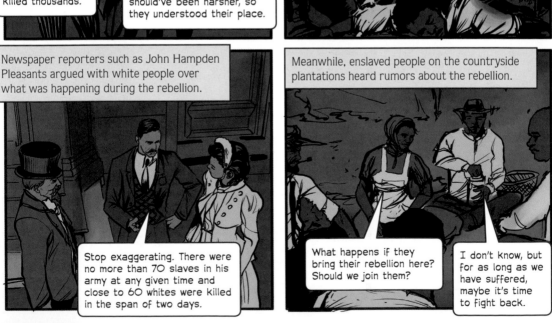

Stop exaggerating. There were no more than 70 slaves in his army at any given time and close to 60 whites were killed in the span of two days.

Meanwhile, enslaved people on the countryside plantations heard rumors about the rebellion.

What happens if they bring their rebellion here? Should we join them?

I don't know, but for as long as we have suffered, maybe it's time to fight back.

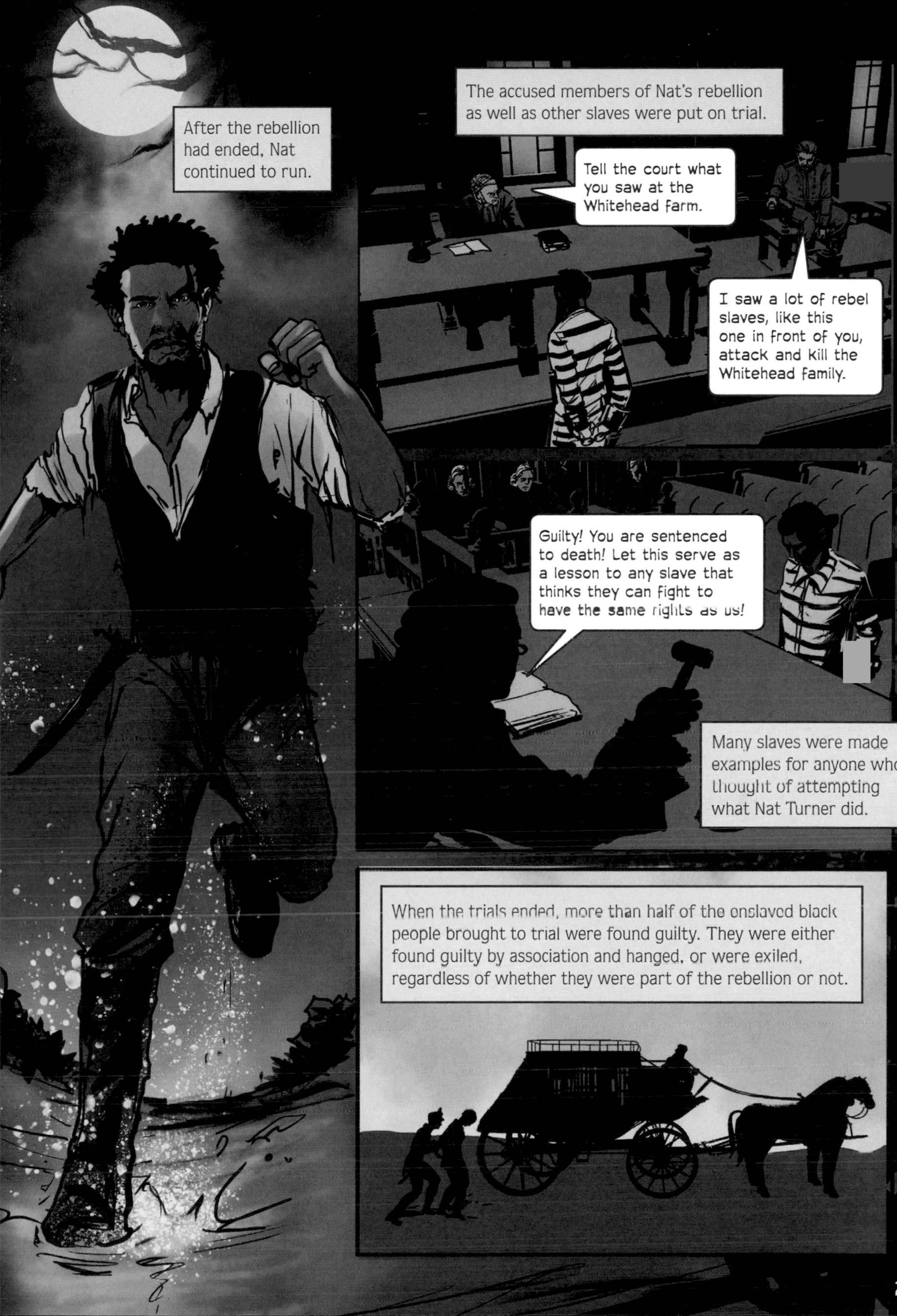
After the rebellion had ended, Nat continued to run.
The accused members of Nat's rebellion as well as other slaves were put on trial.
Tell the court what you saw at the Whitehead farm.
I saw a lot of rebel slaves, like this one in front of you, attack and kill the Whitehead family.
Guilty! You are sentenced to death! Let this serve as a lesson to any slave that thinks they can fight to have the same rights as us!
Many slaves were made examples for anyone who thought of attempting what Nat Turner did.
When the trials ended, more than half of the enslaved black people brought to trial were found guilty. They were either found guilty by association and hanged, or were exiled, regardless of whether they were part of the rebellion or not.

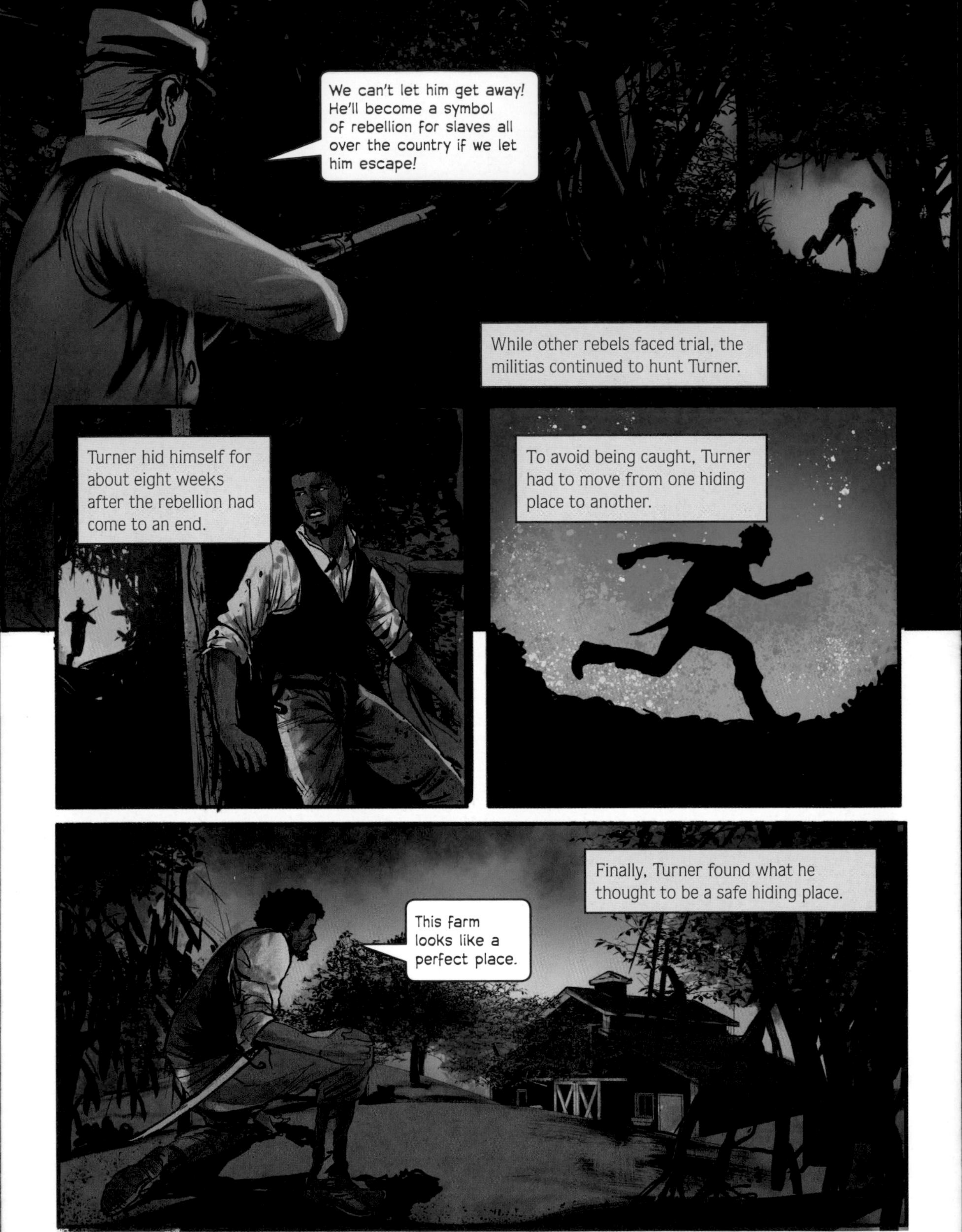
We can't let him get away! He'll become a symbol of rebellion for slaves all over the country if we let him escape!
While other rebels faced trial, the militias continued to hunt Turner.
Turner hid himself for about eight weeks after the rebellion had come to an end.
To avoid being caught, Turner had to move from one hiding place to another.
Finally, Turner found what he thought to be a safe hiding place.
This farm looks like a perfect place.

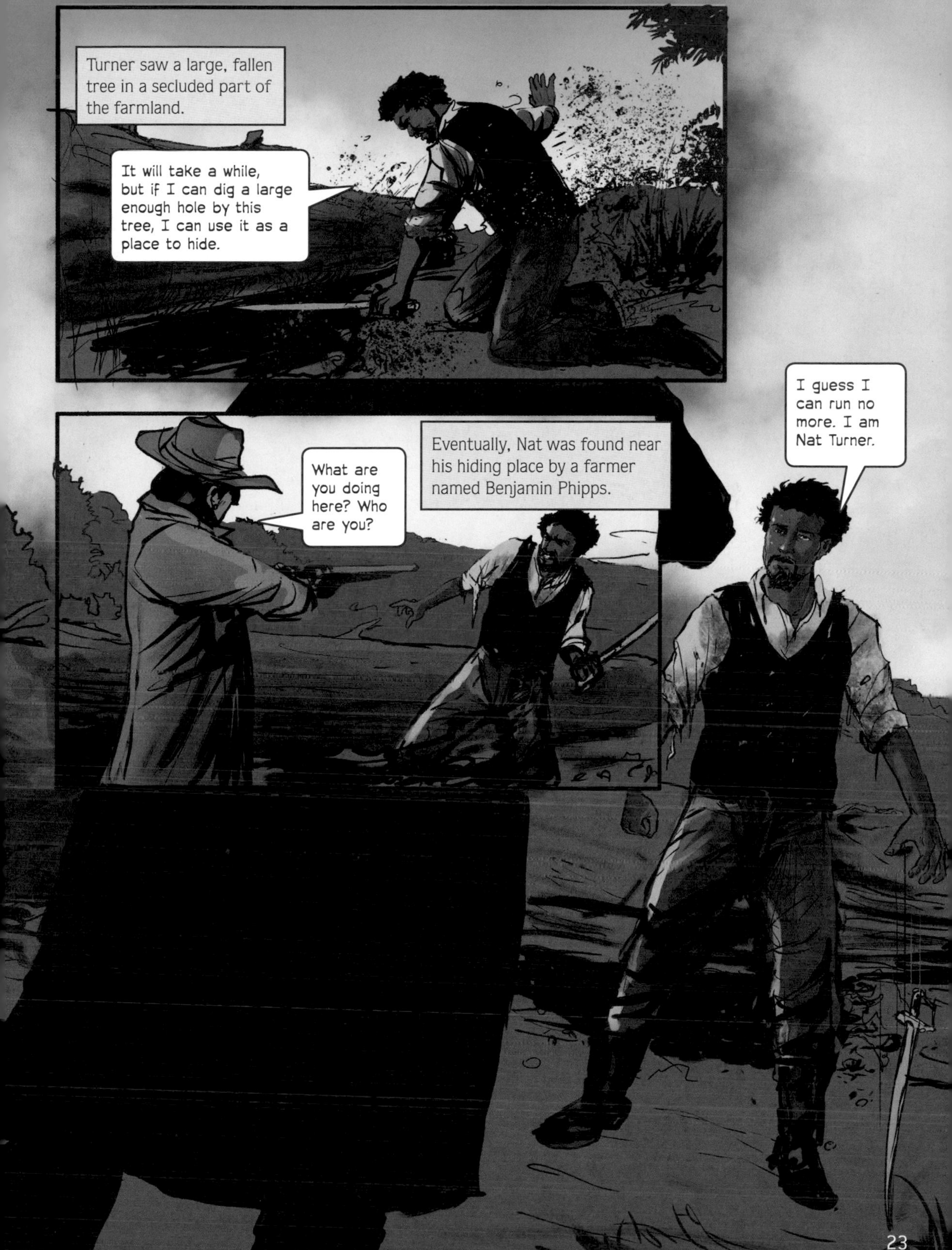

Turner saw a large, fallen tree in a secluded part of the farmland.
It will take a while, but if I can dig a large enough hole by this tree, I can use it as a place to hide.
Eventually, Nat was found near his hiding place by a farmer named Benjamin Phipps.
What are you doing here? Who are you?
I guess I can run no more. I am Nat Turner.

REBELLION'S END

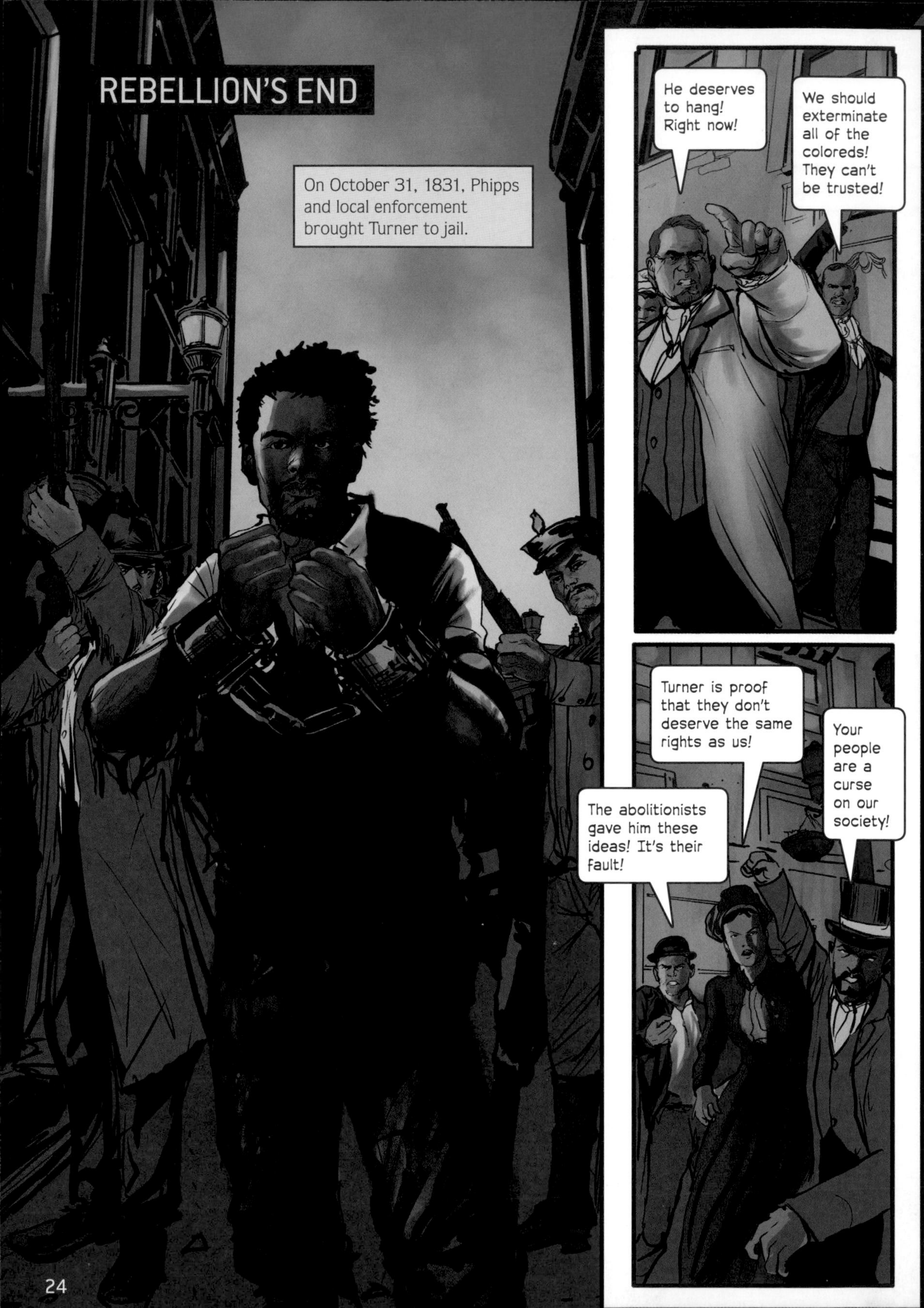
On October 31, 1831, Phipps and local enforcement brought Turner to jail.
He deserves to hang! Right now!
We should exterminate all of the coloreds! They can't be trusted!
Turner is proof that they don't deserve the same rights as us!
Your people are a curse on our society!
The abolitionists gave him these ideas! It's their fault!

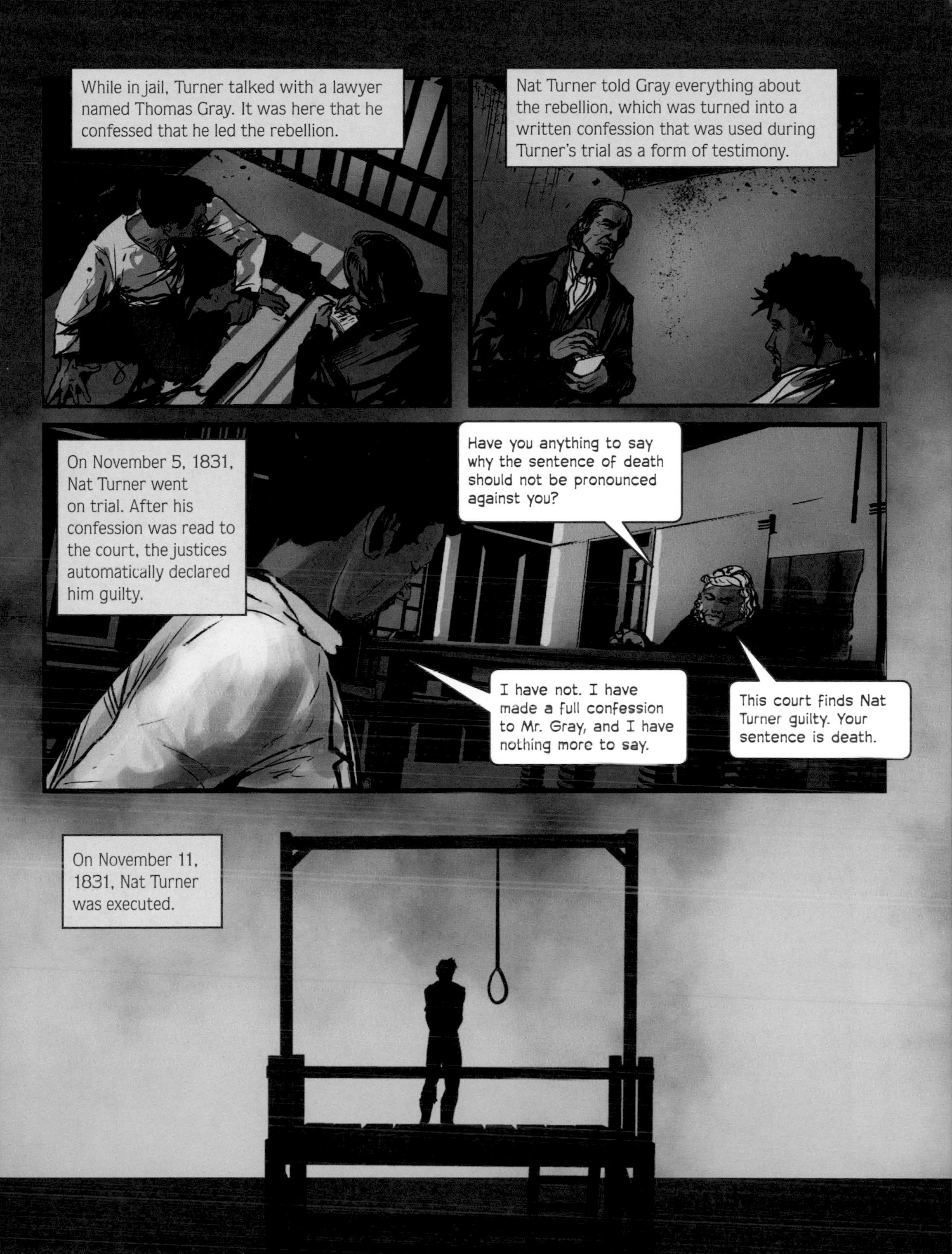

While in jail, Turner talked with a lawyer named Thomas Gray. It was here that he confessed that he led the rebellion.
Nat Turner told Gray everything about the rebellion, which was turned into a written confession that was used during Turner's trial as a form of testimony.
On November 5, 1831, Nat Turner went on trial. After his confession was read to the court, the justices automatically declared him guilty.
Have you anything to say why the sentence of death should not be pronounced against you?
I have not. I have made a full confession to Mr. Gray, and I have nothing more to say.
This court finds Nat Turner guilty. Your sentence is death.
On November 11, 1831, Nat Turner was executed.

Lawmakers, scared of another rebellion began passing new laws regarding the enslaved.

The free black and slave must not have the same freedoms as us. If anything, we must limit them more now.

Virginia Governor John Floyd was concerned that because of Nat Turner, other enslaved black people would start their own revolutions.

Agreed! We must oppress them heavily!

If anything, we must restrict the negro even more. We wish to keep slavery, and we must prevent them from being able to meet, bear arms, and more.

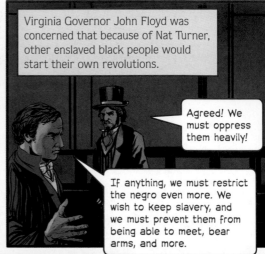

Laws banning blacks from having religious worship, gathering in large groups, or learning how to read or write were enforced.

You are not allowed access to church and there's no preaching allowed!

All I want to do is pass the word of God to my people.

Large groups of you people aren't allowed anymore. Now, break it up before I start shooting.

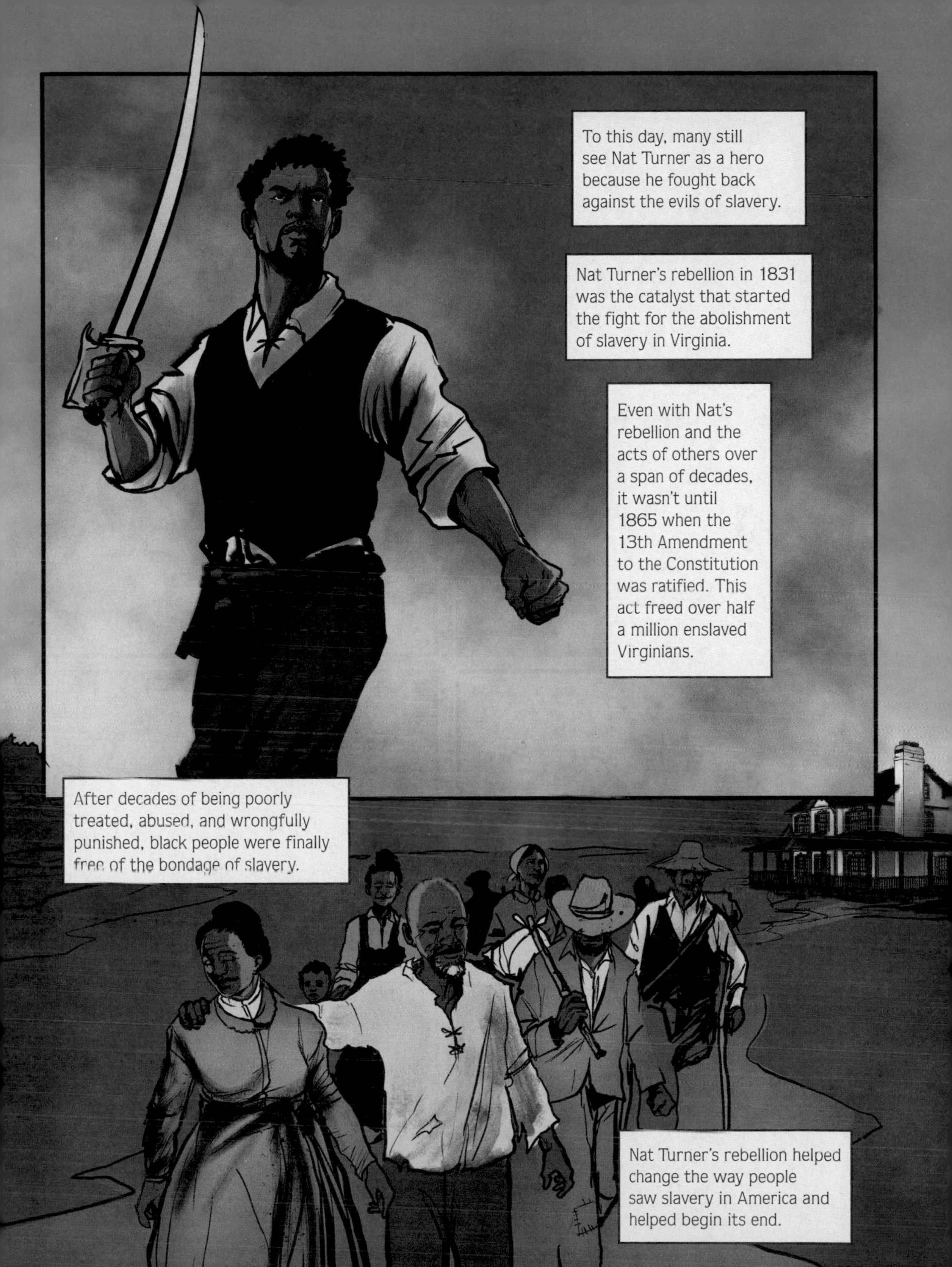
To this day, many still see Nat Turner as a hero because he fought back against the evils of slavery.
Nat Turner's rebellion in 1831 was the catalyst that started the fight for the abolishment of slavery in Virginia.
Even with Nat's rebellion and the acts of others over a span of decades, it wasn't until 1865 when the 13th Amendment to the Constitution was ratified. This act freed over half a million enslaved Virginians.
After decades of being poorly treated, abused, and wrongfully punished, black people were finally free of the bondage of slavery.
Nat Turner's rebellion helped change the way people saw slavery in America and helped begin its end.

MORE ABOUT NAT TURNER'S REBELLION

- Of the 16,000 people who lived in Southampton County, nearly half of them were enslaved people.

- Due to the fears of the rebellion, officials had asked the United States military to help them fight Nat Turner and his men. But by the time the military actually showed up, the rebellion had long ended.

- Many enslaved black people, both men and women, did not agree to follow Turner and his men during the rebellion.

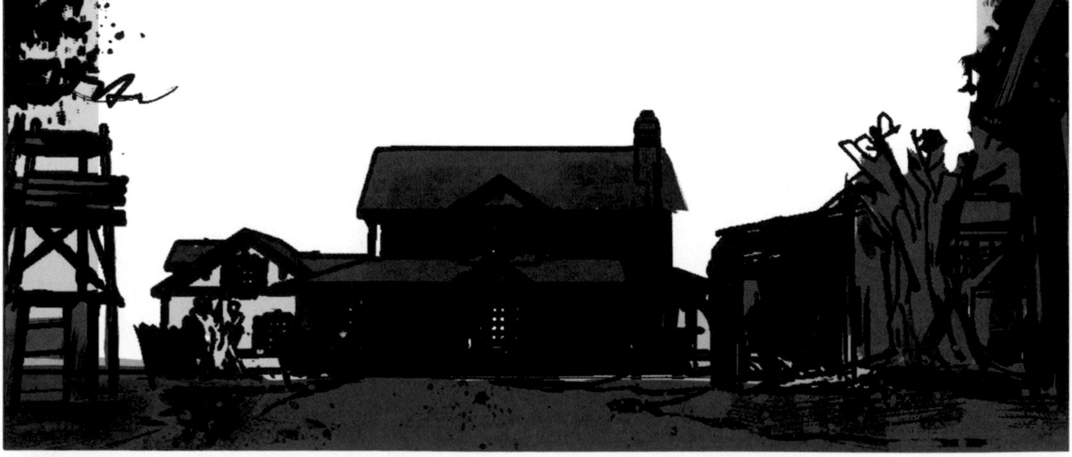

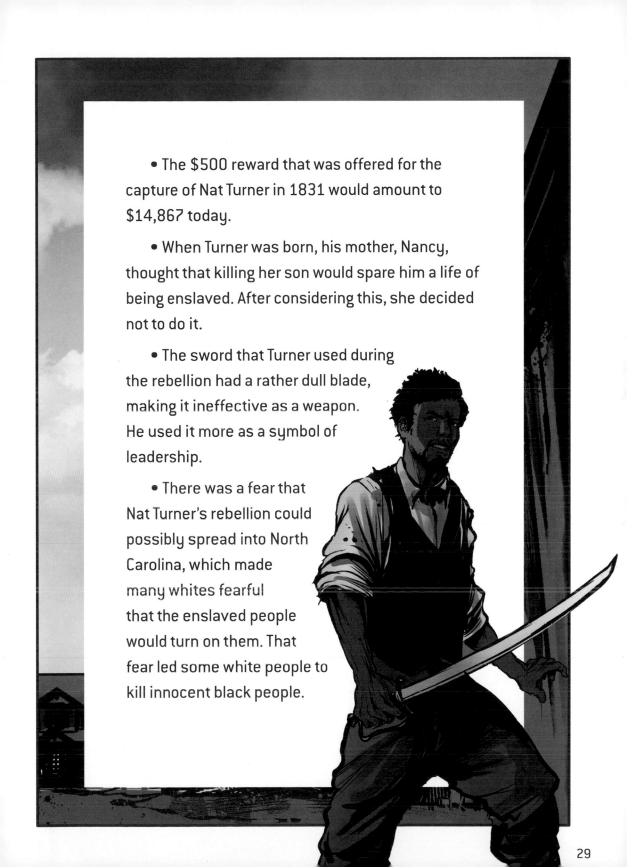

- The $500 reward that was offered for the capture of Nat Turner in 1831 would amount to $14,867 today.

- When Turner was born, his mother, Nancy, thought that killing her son would spare him a life of being enslaved. After considering this, she decided not to do it.

- The sword that Turner used during the rebellion had a rather dull blade, making it ineffective as a weapon. He used it more as a symbol of leadership.

- There was a fear that Nat Turner's rebellion could possibly spread into North Carolina, which made many whites fearful that the enslaved people would turn on them. That fear led some white people to kill innocent black people.

GLOSSARY

abolitionist (ab-uh-LI-shuhn-ist)—a person who worked to end slavery

eclipse (i-KLIPS)—an event in which the moon comes between the sun and the earth, blocking the sun's light

enslaver (en-SLAY-ver)—someone who forces other people to lose their freedom

executed (EK-si-kyoo-ted)—to be put to death

exiled (EG-zahyld)—ordered to leave one's home

heed (HEED)—to listen or understand

militia (muh-LISH-uh)—a group of volunteer citizens who are organized to fight, but are not professional soldiers

oppress (oh-PRESS)—to be treated in a cruel, unjust, and hard way

perish (PAIR-ish)—to die or to be destroyed

prophet (PROF-it)—a person who claims to be a messenger of God

ratified (RAT-uh-fide)—officially approved of

restrict (ri-STRIKT)—to put a limit on or keep under control

salvation (sal-VAY-shuhn)—the saving from danger or evil

testimony (TESS-tuh-moh-nee)—a statement given by a witness who is under oath in a court of law

vision (VIZH-uhn)—a dream or image that conveys a message for an individual

READ MORE

Kawa, Katie. *Slavery Wasn't Only in the South: Exposing Myths About the Civil War*. New York: Gareth Stevens, 2020.

Roxburgh, Ellis. *Nat Turner's Slave Rebellion*. New York: Gareth Stevens, 2018.

Yomtov, Nel. *The Emancipation Proclamation: Asking Tough Questions*. North Mankato, MN: Capstone Press, 2021.

INTERNET SITES

The American Civil War Museum
https://acwm.org/

Civil Rights for Kids: History of Slavery in the United States
https://www.ducksters.com/history/civil_rights/history_of_slavery_in_the_united_states.php

National Museum of African American History & Culture
https://nmaahc.si.edu/

INDEX